THE ART OF
WINE TASTING

THE ART OF

WINE TASTING

AN ILLUSTRATED GUIDEBOOK

by Richard Kinssies

BARNES & NOBLE

NEW YORK

This 2006 edition published by Barnes & Noble Publishing, Inc.
by arrangement with becker&mayer!

Design: Joanna Price
Editorial: Conor Risch
Image Research: Shayna Ian
Production Coordination: Leah Finger
Project Management: Sheila Kamuda

Cover photograph: ©Stockbyte/PictureQuest

2006 Barnes & Noble Publishing

ISBN-13: 978-0-7607-8476-1
ISBN-10: 0-7607-8476-0

Library of Congress Control Number: 2006926049

Printed and bound in China

1 3 5 7 9 10 8 6 4 2

CONTENTS

·····················

INTRODUCTION

One of the great things about wine is that, like art and music, we don't have to know anything about it to enjoy it. We can simply take a sip and decide if it pleases us or not. Beyond that we really don't have to give it another thought. But like art and music, we have the option of pursuing the subject on a different level. For example, we may be indifferent to the music we hear as background sound where we shop or work or live. But that same music may be capable of giving us far greater pleasure if we give it our full attention. Now we can appreciate the nuances and complexities of the performance, and that in turn increases our enjoyment.

It's the same with a bottle of good wine. If we give it some time and attention, we are much more likely to appreciate it beyond the simple pleasure of its tasting good. Given the opportunity, even a modest wine can reveal character and uniqueness that would have otherwise gone unnoticed.

One of the most informative and fun ways of getting to know a bottle of wine (or several) is to gather a few friends together to taste and discuss it. Like a book at a book club, a wine at a wine tasting can reveal more detail when several people offer their insights and perspectives.

In this wine-tasting kit we have assembled the

essential items and provided the necessary information for you to easily host a tasting party.

But this kit represents more than just an event. We have also included valuable information presented in simple, easy-to-understand terms on how to taste wine just like the pros. You'll see that it's not so hard to do, and once learned, it's something you'll always be able to draw upon. Perhaps the most significant lesson learned by anyone attending a wine tasting, however, is the realization that a glass of wine has the power not only to give individual pleasure but to create lasting friendships. It's hard to put a value on that.

Happy tasting!

CHAPTER ONE

IN THE BEGINNING: THE GRAPE

There is an essential philosophical difference between European and New World winemaking that is important for us to understand.

In Europe, the Old World, a wine is judged on how well it represents the place where the wine was made. A wine from Burgundy, France, for example, is not judged on how much it tastes like Pinot Noir (the exclusive red grape of Burgundy) but on how well it represents the village or vineyard where the grapes were grown. This concept is known as *terroir,* and it's the cornerstone of European wine production. It originates from centuries of trial-and-error efforts to produce the very best wines a place has to offer. It includes matching the vineyard sites that have the best soils, altitude, and exposure to the sun with a particular grape best suited to those conditions. In addition, over many generations the winemakers honed their vineyard practices and winemaking techniques to coax the best from each vine.

Eventually these specific sites and the areas around them began to exhibit a sense of place that distinguished them from other wine areas even a short distance away. As time went on this became the standard by which the quality of a wine was

Syrah grapes produce wines of varying complexity depending on the growing climate.

measured. The French base their *Appellation d' Origine Contrôlée* system on these very principles. It's the reason that most wines in France and throughout Europe are named for the place the grapes were grown and not for the grape from which the wine was made.

Conversely, in the New World, which includes North America, South America, South Africa, New Zealand, and Australia, a wine is judged on how well it behaves like the grape from which it was made. A merlot from the Napa Valley, then, is not judged on how well it tastes like a Napa Valley wine but solely on its merits as a merlot. As a result, New World wines are usually named for the grape used to make the wine. (Federal law requires that a wine contain at least seventy-five percent of the grape named on the label.)

The reason the New World, led by the United States, approached wine production from this entirely different perspective is that winemakers here did not have centuries of tradition and trial and error to guide their wine industry. Nor did they have the cultural wine-drinking habits that Europe had. Keep in mind that buying, selling, and consuming wine was a crime here for thirteen years during Prohibition. The New World wine industry only began to take shape after World War II.

But what the New World did have was innovation and technology, and it applied them with earnest. New vineyard techniques and winemaking technology, including temperature-controlled fermenting tanks, helped bring wine production out of its dark age. And the whole world has benefited.

Today, the "terroirists" of the Old World and the technologists of the New are slowly melding philosophies. French wine growers, for example, use stainless-steel tanks that are temperature-controlled and run by computers. They have also put into practice many of the vineyard innovations discovered by Australians and Americans. For their part, the New World wine growers now pay special attention to each vineyard site and do what is necessary to preserve those distinctions in the wine. It is not an overstatement to say that because of the bringing together of these two strong and relevant philo- sophies, the world has entered into what can only be considered a Golden Age of wine production.

Although there are literally hundreds of varieties of wine grapes and then more hundreds of clones within the varieties, here is a short list with brief profiles of the wine grapes you'll most likely encounter. Names in parentheses are commonly used synonyms for the grapes.

We've also listed several descriptors used to identify the aromas and flavors exhibited by each grape. However, understand that the specific characteristics of each varietal will vary with each vineyard, region, and winemaking method. Don't expect to experience all of the descriptors listed, or that you won't encounter new ones.

RED GRAPES

Cabernet Sauvignon

Descriptors: Cassis, green olive, bell pepper, mint, raspberry, chocolate, coffee.

Cabernet Sauvignon is the king of the red wine grapes. At its best it can produce wines of amazing complexity and structure that can mature and improve for decades after bottling.

Adding to its allure and credibility is the fact that many of the most distinguished, expensive, and collectible red table wines are made entirely or partly from Cabernet Sauvignon. The most famous examples come from its native turf—Bordeaux, France—and the Napa Valley, but it's grown successfully throughout the wine world in warmer climates. Because it can be a bit tight and closed in its youth, it is often blended with other grapes, especially Merlot, to soften its edges, add fruitiness, and increase its complexity.

The Cabernet Sauvignon is the most famous of the red grapes, producing many of the world's most sought-after wines.

Merlot

Descriptors: Plum, cassis, cherry.

Merlot enjoys a similar reputation for quality as Cabernet Sauvignon, but seldom reaches the same heights. Wines from Merlot are softer and fruitier than those from Cabernet Sauvignon and mature earlier—both on the vine and in the bottle. As Merlot is often used to soften Cabernet Sauvignon, Cab is often blended into Merlot to give it more structure and backbone.

Pinot Noir

Descriptors: Cherry, clove, cinnamon, black pepper.

Often referred to as the "heartbreak grape" because of its difficulty to grow, Pinot Noir can produce wines of stunning complexity, especially from the vineyards of its native Burgundy, France, where it's the only red grape allowed. Wines from Pinot Noir are often lighter in color and body than other red grapes (they have thinner skins and lack at least one of the hues that make up the color red). Pinot prefers a cool growing environment and has done well in cooler areas of California, Oregon's Willamette Valley, and it shows great promise in New Zealand. One of its finest contributions is to the great sparkling wines of Champagne, France, where it contributes body, aroma, and, some would argue, the finest of character to the wines.

Syrah (Shiraz)

Descriptors: Black pepper, white pepper, blackberry, clove, dark chocolate.

Syrah is rapidly becoming the darling of consumers and critics alike. It's a rugged red grape that can make good wine in a wide range of growing conditions. In hotter climates, like that of its home in France's northern Rhone Valley, Syrah can produce powerful and complex wines brimming with fruit and spice. In cooler climates, wines from Syrah tend to be less complex, fruitier, and less powerful, but still worthwhile. So far its best sites outside of France are Australia (where it's known as Shiraz), Tuscany, South Africa, California, and Washington.

Zinfandel (Plavic Mali, Primativo)

Descriptors: Raspberry, black pepper, weeds, prune, raisin.

Introduced to California in the 1850s, Zinfandel was a favorite of the Italian immigrants there because it made rustic wines reminiscent of those back in Italy. Some of those gnarly original vines still survive today and can produce magnificent wines. For a century and a half, California claimed Zinfandel as its own because no one knew its origin, but through recent DNA testing this mystery grape was found to have originated in Croatia, where it's still grown under the name Plavic Mali. It's also grown in southern Italy, where it's called Primativo. Lately some very good zinfandels have come out of Washington.

The versatile Cabernet Franc is frequently blended with other grapes, but it also produces excellent wines of its own.

Sangiovese

Descriptors: Cherry, currants.

This is the workhorse red grape of Italy. It excels in the region of Tuscany, where it's the main ingredient of chianti and other wines. At its best it produces wines with bright fruit flavor and zesty acidity. California producers have tried their hand at Sangiovese with limited success. Too often winemakers treat this rather delicate grape like Cabernet Sauvignon by leaving it too long on the vine and then subjecting it to too much new oak when it's barreled. Some even blend in too high a proportion of Cabernet or Zinfandel (dubbing the wine "Zingiovese"). The result is often a wine that more resembled Cab or Zin than Sangiovese. But improvements are being made.

Grenache

Descriptors: Plum, cherry, spice, blueberry, blackberry.

Producers in the southern Rhône Valley depend on Grenache to provide the backbone to their wines, which can be made with up to a dozen different varieties. It's also one of the most important red grapes in Spain and has grown in popularity in California, as have all Rhône varieties. Grenache gives red wines of enormous fruit and also makes excellent rosé wines.

Cabernet Franc

Descriptors: Raspberry, blueberry.

This is one of the most important red grapes in France, especially in the Loire Valley, where it rules as the dominant red varietal contributing to red, rosé, and even sparkling wines. It's also important in Bordeaux, where it's one of the five red grapes allowed in the appellation. In the United States, as in Bordeaux, it's often blended with other grapes, especially Merlot, with which it seems to get along very well. But over the past few years, U.S. producers have more frequently sold it as a single varietal.

WHITE GRAPES

Chardonnay

Descriptors: Green apple, yellow apple, tropical fruits (banana, coconut, pineapple).

As Cabernet Sauvignon is king of the red grapes, Chardonnay is queen of the whites. Arguably the finest white wines made are those from Chardonnay grapes, specifically the great whites from Burgundy,

France, which are made exclusively from Chardonnay. It's also the only white grape planted in the Champagne region of France, where it makes up a third of all vineyards and contributes its elegance to these magnificent sparkling wines. However ubiquitous, and no matter how much mediocre wine is made from Chardonnay, it still remains the most revered of all white grapes.

Sauvignon Blanc (Fumé Blanc)

Descriptors: Lime, grapefruit, grass, gooseberry, hay, asparagus, mineral.

This is one of the most distinctive of all the white grapes. Depending on how the grapes are grown and treated in the winery, the resultant wines can be either fresh, clean, grassy, mineral, and citrus, or full and lush with oak and butter flavors. Sauvignon Blanc is a varietal that originated in France, where it makes the crisp and fragrant wines of Sancerre, and contributes to the dry wines of Bordeaux and the sweet, honeyed dessert wines of Sauternes. It also does very well in the cool Marlborough region of New Zealand as well as the West Coast of the United States. As long as a sauvignon blanc wine isn't too laden with oak flavors (a common abuse of this grape), it can match up to an amazing array of foods.

Chenin Blanc

Descriptors: Green apple, yellow apple, honeydew melon, pear.

Chenin Blanc is one of the most underrated of the white wine grapes. The reason is undoubtedly that so much sweetish, inexpensive wine has been made in the name of this grape that it's nearly futile for producers to go thorough the trouble to make and market more expensive efforts. But anyone who has tasted a decades-old chenin from France's Loire Valley will experience an epiphany as to the potential of this noble grape. It yields wines of high acidity with lots of fruit and can be made bone-dry or, if left on the vine to over-ripen, sweet and luscious as honey. Good chenin can age for fifty years or more.

Pinot Gris (Pinot Grigio)

Descriptors: Pear, melon.

Wines from Pinot Gris, which is the gray (*gris* or *grigio*) relative of the Pinot Noir, make up the fastest-growing category of white wine in the world. It's called Pinot Gris in Alsace, France, where it produces the classic versions, and Pinot Grigio in northern Italy, where oceans of pretty good wine are being produced and shipped primarily to the United States. It also excels in northern Oregon and in certain areas of California and Washington.

Riesling

Descriptors: Green apple, lemon, peach, apricot, honey, floral.

The Riesling is the most overlooked and undervalued of any grape—capable of producing astonishingly elegant and complex wines, which can be bone-dry, slightly sweet, or lusciously sweet dessert wines. Well-made sweet Riesling can live indefinitely, and even the dry versions are capable of aging for decades. The best Rieslings come from Germany, Alsace, France, Australia, and often Washington.

Viognier

Descriptors: Pear, peach, apricot.

Still a rather obscure white grape, Viognier has been able to ride the wave of fascination for Rhône Valley grapes and has managed to create and maintain a dedicated and growing following. Though it can make sweet, dessert-style wines, it most often is made into a full-bodied table wine with light aromas and full flavors.

Gewürztraminer

Descriptors: Grapefruit, lichee, pineapple, floral.

Pungently aromatic Gewürztraminer can make some truly exotic wines with enticing aromas of lichees, flowers, and grapefruit. It can be made either dry or sweet. Though it's grown throughout the world, it's at its best in Alsace, France.

Riesling rules in Germany, where some of the best wines from this grape are produced.

CHAPTER TWO

HOW WINE IS MADE

In the days and weeks prior to harvest, the winemaker and the grape grower constantly prowl the vineyards to check the condition of the grapes. It's critical that the fruit be harvested at the right moment if the best wine is to be made. Measurements of the sugars and acids are taken in the field and in the lab to determine when these important components are in perfect balance. They also taste the grapes because they know that even though the numbers from the lab may say it's time to pick, the grapes must also taste ripe. Then, when all conditions are just so, the decision is made to harvest, and the winemaking begins.

Here are the general procedures followed by winemakers to turn clusters of grapes into bottles of wine. Within this group of tasks lie a myriad of winemaking minutia that can be employed to customize a wine, but these are the basics.

Processing the Grapes

After harvesting, grapes need to be processed before fermentation can begin. Depending on the type or style of wine to be made, the grapes will undergo one or more of several procedures.

Stemming/Crushing

The first procedure is to remove the grapes from their stems and crush or break the skins so that the juice inside can be released. This is usually done with a machine aptly called a stemmer/crusher. There are several versions, but they all perform the same function. The grape clusters are forced through the holes of a mesh or screen, which breaks the skins as they go through. The stems won't fit through the holes, so they stay behind. The crushed grapes and their juice (now called "must") are collected in a receptacle below the stemmer/crusher and are now ready for the next step.

At this point it's important to know that the juice of virtually all grapes is clear and all color pigments are stored in the skin. White wines are seldom fermented with their skins, while red wines always are so that the color can be extracted from the skins. It's interesting to note that as long as the juice is kept away from the skins, it's possible to produce a white or pink wine from black grapes (think white Zinfandel).

The Press

If a white wine is going to be made, the next step is to pump the crushed grapes into a wine press where the remaining juice can be extracted. Though the traditional and picturesque wooden-slatted basket press with a large screw down the middle is still used, nowadays a computer-controlled bladder press usually does the job. Here, the must is pumped into the press, which contains a large rubber bladder very much like an inner tube in a tire. The bladder will inflate to exert just the right amount of pressure to squeeze the juice from the pulp without damaging the seeds. Damaged seeds can impart bitterness to a wine.

A red wine, by the way, will undergo its turn in the press after the fermentation is complete.

Fermentation

From the press, the relatively clear juice for a white wine will now be pumped into fermenting tanks. If a red wine is to be made, the entire lot—juice, skins, seeds, pulp, and all—goes directly into the fermenting tank from the stemmer/crusher.

The winemaker will now add a yeast mixture to the must, and fermentation will begin.

An easy way to understand what happens during

fermentation is to remember this simple formula: $S + Y = E = A/CO_2$. Translated, it means sugar (S) gets eaten by yeasts (Y), which secrete enzymes (E) as waste, which cause a chemical reaction in the must, creating alcohol (A) and carbon dioxide (CO_2).

White wines are usually fermented at lower temperatures than red wines to preserve their aromas and fruitiness, while red wines need more heat to extract all they can from the skins.

During red wine fermentation, the skins and pulp are naturally forced to the surface and form a firm mass called a "cap." But it's the stuff inside this cap that will give the red wine its color and character so different methods have been devised to keep the cap in as much contact with the must as possible. One of the most basic methods used is called "punching down" whereby a long pole with a short perpendicular block at its end is used to break up the cap and push it back into the must. Punching down can be done several times a day during fermentation. Another method is called "pumping over." Here a hose is attached to a spigot near the bottom outside of the tank, and wine is pumped onto the cap. Sometimes both methods are used.

Fermentation can last anywhere from five days to several weeks, and in some exceptional cases several years, but usually the job is done after a week or so. Fermentation will stop:

1. When the yeasts have eaten all the sugar
2. When the yeasts are killed by the alcohol they have created, or alcohol is added to the must to stop fermentation, as in the making of port wine

3. If the temperature generated by the process climbs too high for the yeasts to survive

4. If the temperature drops and the yeasts go dormant

Clarification

After the fermentation process is complete, the next issue is to clarify the wine by removing the lees. Lees are the debris of fermentation including all the little bodies of those yeasts that have given their lives for the cause, as well as various flotsams.

There are three primary methods of clarifying a wine: racking, fining, and filtering. Cold stabilization is used to remove excess tartaric acid.

Racking is simply waiting for the lees to settle to the bottom of a tank or barrel and then transferring the clear wine to a clean tank or barrel. Racking is the original and simplest method of clarification. All efforts to clarify a wine beyond racking are optional (though most winemakers use at least one or the other).

Fining is the procedure by which a clarifying agent is added to the wine. In days gone by, bull's blood was used, as were whipped egg whites. Bull's blood is thankfully a thing of the past, though egg whites are occasionally used today. Most winemakers now use fining agents designed for the task that are more effective and economical.

When fining a wine, the winemaker will add the fining agent, then wait for it to coagulate any particulates in the wine and sink to the bottom of the tank or barrel before racking the wine.

Filtering is the use of a machine to clarify a wine. In this method, the wine is forced through a series of filter pads or spun in a centrifuge until it's clear.

Cold stabilization is covered on page 44.

Making Sparkling Wines

Sparkling wines are made by causing a still wine (one without bubbles) to ferment a second time. During the first fermentation, the carbon dioxide gas created by the yeasts is allowed to escape into the atmosphere. But during this second fermentation for a sparkling wine, the vessel that holds the fermenting wine is sealed so that the carbon dioxide gas remains in the wine.

This second fermentation takes place either in a large tank or in individual bottles. In either case a

measured amount of sugar and yeasts are added to a still wine. That wine is put into the vessel, which is then sealed and the fermentation begins.

The bottle method is the original one innovated in the Champagne region of France several hundred years ago by Benedictine monks led by Pierre (Dom) Perignon. It's known today as the "classic" or "Champagne" method.

For the classic method, after the second fermentation is completed in the bottle, the wine is allowed to rest on its lees (sometimes for years), which can impart desirable aromas, flavors, and complexities to the wine. After lees contact is complete, the wine undergoes a slow, methodical process (mostly involving carefully shaking and spinning the bottles) designed to coax the lees into the neck of the bottle. The neck of the bottle is then frozen and the cork removed, releasing the icy plug of lees and leaving a clear wine. The fill level of the bottle is then adjusted before being recorked, labeled, and allowed to rest for a few months before being shipped for sale.

This method is expensive, time-consuming, and labor-intensive, usually taking between one and five years before the wine is available for sale.

With the tank method, referred to as the "bulk process" or "Charmat" method after the man who invented it, the wine undergoes its second fermentation in a sealed tank. After fermentation, there is no lees contact, and the wine is immediately pumped through a filter and into bottles. This method is very fast and economical, with wines ready for sale in a matter of weeks instead of years.

The classic method produces the finest sparkling wines, although there are some very fine examples made by variations of the Charmat method, such as the Prosecco wines from northern Italy.

DID YOU KNOW?

Champagnes are classified as Brut, Extra Sec, Sec, and Demi-Sec according to their sugar content—Brut being the driest Champagne and Demi-Sec the sweetest.

CHAPTER THREE

HOW TO TASTE WINE

Drinking or Tasting

It's easy to drink wine—we just put it in our mouths and swallow. However, the most we can expect to learn from the experience is whether or not we like the wine. Maybe that's all we care to know. Fair enough.

Tasting wine, on the other hand, is different in that we want the wine to reveal more about itself. We want to be able to "read" a wine. We want to differentiate between a good wine and a better wine, and to decide for ourselves if an expensive wine is worth the money, or if it deserved the high score it received in the press. Ultimately, we just want to trust our own palates so that we can make our own decisions.

But to many of us, the idea of acquiring these skills is daunting. Wine seems to evoke such a sense of awe that some of us believe tasting wine takes special powers or is a sort of dark art revealed only to chosen initiates. But anyone can learn to taste wine. Sure, there are a few procedures to learn, but then it's just practice, practice, practice. Actually, there is one secret to becoming a good wine taster. Without it, you can only aspire to proficiency.

The secret is concentration. Concentrating on the wine being tasted is what separates the good tasters from all others.

Notes

It's important that you take notes on the wines you taste. And the sooner you get started, the better. Collected notes can serve as an anthology of the important wines you've tasted in the same way a photo album can hold the significant moments in your life. Notes can also give you a practical reference to the wines you have tasted and help you recall your impressions. They may say only that you liked or disliked a wine, but that may be very useful information for your next trip to the wine shop. There is also another very important reason for

DID YOU KNOW?

Poor weather during a growing season can result in a harvest of grapes that are lacking enough natural sugars to ferment properly. To counter this, some winemakers use a process called "chaptalization," wherein sugars are added to the must during fermentation ensuring a correct alcohol level in the vintage.

jotting down your thoughts as you taste, even if you never keep your notes. Writing notes forces you to organize and focus your thoughts and concentrate on what it is you are tasting. And we know that concentration is key to being a good wine taster.

A notes section is included in the back of this book to help you get started on a personal wine journal. When you fill it, up you can use other wine journals available at bookstores. A three-ring binder or spiral notebook will also work. We've also included two notepads in the kit with sheets that you and your guests can tear off and use to gather your thoughts during the tasting.

When taking notes, it's a good idea to keep to the chronology of the tasting procedures. This will help you stay focused. Comment on the appearance, smell, taste, and overall impressions of the wine, in that order. Be brief and only jot down the highlights of a wine, things that will help you remember it later. A word or two will do. By way of example, here's how your notes on a dessert wine might read:

Bright, pale gold color. Lush nose of honey, butter, orange blossoms. Rich flavors of butter, dried apricots, fig, and honey with a long toffee finish. The wine was luscious, sweet, and balanced. My favorite of the tasting.

Describing Wines

One of the great pleasures of tasting fine wine is sharing the experience. But the problem with sharing a wine experience is the fact that taste is abstract. We cannot point to a smell or a flavor and comment on it. Instead we must describe what it is we are smelling and tasting, and that may not always be easy. Think of how you would describe the flavor of salt, for example, to someone who had never tasted salt before. If you could not use the descriptor "salty," it would be virtually impossible. Luckily, wines can taste and smell like other things, and by making references to those things we can convey our impressions.

To make it easy for you, we have included a flavor wheel in your kit, which is commonly used in the wine industry to train tasters. It's broken down like a pie chart into categories of possible smells you may encounter in wine. It should also be used for finding descriptors for taste. It is a very useful tool for learning how to describe wines, so take the time to study it. Refer to it either actually or mentally whenever you taste wine.

It's essential, however, that you look beyond the flavor wheel for your descriptors. The wheel is not intended to, nor could it possibly, cover every descriptor that every wine has to offer. Rather, look to the wheel for categories of aroma and flavor, and as a tool to stimulate your imagination when you work to find the right descriptor.

The Procedures for Tasting Wine

When tasting wines we use all of our senses: sight, smell, taste, and even touch and hearing. Though the thought of touching or hearing a wine may seem odd, both of these senses do play a role when enjoying a wine. For touch, consider the texture, the weight, and even the temperature of a wine. And what about the feeling of all those bubbles when you taste a sparkling wine? For hearing, think about the pop of a cork, the glug of wine being poured, the sound of champagne bubbles, or the clink of a glass. With the exception of texture and weight, we don't spend much time pondering these senses, but it's important to be aware of them and realize that they each add to the pleasure of the experience. Our main focus, though, will be on the senses of sight, smell, and taste.

When you approach a glass of wine for tasting, it's important to think about each sense individually. And just like when writing your notes, it's best to employ each of the following steps in the same order every time you taste a wine. Eventually, just like driving a car, you won't even have to think about what to do.

Here is the procedure for tasting wine.

LOOK

When we look at a wine, we should turn the glass on its side. This will spread the wine out and give you a better perspective. It helps to hold the glass against a stark white background such as a napkin or piece of paper. Good lighting is also important—a wine tasting is not the place for mood lighting.

When we look at a wine, we should think about two things: color and clarity.

Color: Color offers clues to the type or style of the wine and its condition. Let's say the wine is brown. If it's a chardonnay or a riesling, we may have a problem. But if it's sherry or marsala, then the wine is as it should be, or "true to type."

White wines, which are not all white, range from

neutral to pale green or pale yellow, to straw and lemon, and on to golden. The darker the color in all wines, the more intense the wine. Remember, though, that intensity has little to do with complexity, which is the true measure of great wine.

Young red wines can be dark and opaque and may have a bluish or purplish tint. This will diminish as the wine ages. Older reds will become more translucent with a tawny or onionskin hue.

All wines age to brown. White wines will darken as they oxidize (like a sliced apple), and red wines will lighten to brown as color and tannins drop out of the wine (creating sediment at the bottom of the bottle).

Clarity: With the state of modern winemaking, most wines are bright and clear, but occasionally something may appear in your glass that will get your attention. The first thing to remember is that nothing in the wine will harm you if ingested. The issue here is aesthetics.

Sometimes bits of cork may be floating in your wine. This is not the fault of the wine. The cork could be old or crumbly, or perhaps it was caused by the corkscrew—or more likely, operator error. If it's off-putting or there is quite a bit of it floating in your glass, decant the wine into a clean glass. Otherwise, consider the cork dust as a good source of fiber.

Tartrate crystals can appear on the end of the cork or collect at the bottom of the bottle. They can look like sugar, salt, or even shards of glass, but they are simply the excess tartaric acid in the wine that has crystallized (see explanation on page 46).

These crystals are odorless, colorless, and tasteless, and will not harm you in any way. The appearance of tartrate crystals indicates that the winemaker chose not to cold-stabilize the wine. Many winemakers feel that the less that is done to a wine, the better off the wine will be.

Sediment in red wines is probably the most likely source of cloudiness in a wine. Older red wines or those that have not been fined or filtered (see page 28) may throw some sediment. A small amount of sediment is no big deal, but lots of the stuff can make a wine look murky and unattractive. It can even feel gritty in your mouth and can spoil an otherwise pleasant tasting experience. The best defense against sediment is to prevent it from getting into the glass in the first place.

If a wine has severe sediment (to check, simply hold the bottle up to the light), stand it up before opening it so that the particles can settle to the bottom of the bottle. This may take a few hours or a day or more. Then carefully open the wine and pour it slowly (no "glugging") into a decanter or clean glass water pitcher leaving the sediment and a small amount of the wine in the bottle.

Remember that whatever color and clarity the wine reveals, it's only an indication of the condition and character of a wine. Withhold judgment until you have smelled and tasted the wine.

SMELL

Smell is the most important sense we use when analyzing wines. The human olfactory system is

capable of detecting more than nine thousand different smells or aromas. By contrast, we can distinguish only four tastes. The combination of aroma and taste creates flavor. So, without smell there would be no flavor.

Wines smell (and taste) like other things, which is a great help when describing wines. They can smell like flowers, fruits, herbs, spices, and oak—among many others (refer to the flavor wheel in your kit).

Remember that these sensations occur naturally in the wine. With the exception of the aromas and flavors of new oak barrels, nothing has been added to impart specific aromas or flavors.

White and red wines each have their own particular set of smells. The floral smell in white wines is often of blossoms. Fruity aromas often resemble melons, stone fruits, pears, or apples. For red wines, the smell of flowers may be of roses or violets, and the fruity aromas may be of red fruits such as cherries, strawberries, or raspberries, or black fruits such as blackberries or currants.

To get all the aromas the wine has to offer, always swirl the glass before you sniff. This agitates the wine and causes it to release aromas. Now draw in a long deep sniff, and concentrate on what it is you smell. If you need to, look at your flavor wheel (now your aroma wheel) for clues and be as specific as you can. Is the wine fruity? If so, what kind of fruit? Apples? What kind of apples? A Granny Smith is very different from a Golden Delicious. Smell the wine several times, and jot down your notes before moving on to tasting. Remember to concentrate.

TASTE

We have four tastes. On the tip of the tongue we perceive sweetness. Midway back on each side of the tongue we taste acidity/sourness and salt. On the back of the tongue bitterness is detected. These four tastes combine with smell to create flavor.

We experience three phases of taste when we put wine in our mouths. It's important to know these phases so that we can get the most out of tasting a wine. They are the attack, the evolution, and the finish (the French invented these terms).

Attack: This is the initial impact of the components of acid, sugar, tannin, and alcohol on your palate. Components have no flavor, but they affect how the wine behaves in your mouth. For a full explanation, please refer to page 44. The attack should last for about two to three seconds.

Evolution: This is when flavors begin to develop or "evolve" on the palate. Now it's time to consider what flavors the wine is showing. Refer to your flavor wheel. Go through the same procedures you did when you smelled the wine. Make sure you roll the wine all around in your mouth. The evolution should last another three to four seconds beyond the attack.

Finish: This is the flavor that lingers after the wine has been spit out or swallowed. After spitting or swallowing the wine, breathe out slowly through your nose with your mouth closed. You'll taste the wine on the back of your palate. Allow several seconds for your impressions of the finish to develop.

SPIT

After the wine has given its all, swallow it or spit it out. Spitting is necessary if you are tasting many wines for analysis (at a wine tasting or on a tour of wineries), or if you otherwise don't want to consume wine. It may sound unattractive or wasteful, but it can be the right thing to do. All the pros do it. You may feel awkward at first, but you'll get the hang of it. Just keep napkins at the ready.

THINK

By now, the wine should have revealed itself to you. You have noted its appearance, its smell, and its flavors, and you should have enough information to write down your overall impressions. Remember that a wine is more than the sum of its parts. It isn't all violets and cherries and oak. Ask yourself if the wine is simple or complex. The best wines are nuanced and layered with many subtle characters. Are the flavors long on the palate? What about the texture and weight? How does the wine compare with the others being tasted? Also consider how the wine would pair with food. Keep in mind that wines will change as they are exposed to oxygen, so it's a good idea to retaste the wine and be prepared to alter your conclusions.

The Components of Wine

Components are an important part of the makeup of any wine, yet too often tasters simply ignore them.

The reason is that most of us are just not aware of what components are or how they affect the personality of a wine.

Components function as the skeletal structure of a wine. They are the framework onto which everything else is attached to create a complete wine. Wines are made up of many components, the most abundant being water, but we are going to concentrate on the four most important ones for tasting wine, which are acid, tannin, sugar, and alcohol. The object when tasting a wine is to discern the balance of these components—that is, their proper relationship to each other and to the wine as a whole.

Though components can affect the way a wine will taste, they have no, or very little, discernable flavor of their own. So, when considering components, don't look for flavor, but for intensity and balance. Remember that to one person a spike of tartness from acidity may be pleasing, while to another it can be off-putting. Because there is no correct balance for these components, each of us has to rely on our own subjective assessment of the wine, which means we can't be wrong.

ACID

Acid functions as the nervous system of the wine. It gives it its life. A wine short on acid will be flabby and flat like a soda without fizz.

Acid gives the wine its tartness or sourness, and can affect the perception of sweetness in a wine. A wine high in residual sugar (unfermented sugars) will be in need of higher acids than a dry wine. If the acids are not kicked up in sweet wines, the wines may appear heavy and dull like cough syrup.

Higher-acid wines match very well with food by cutting through fats and cleansing and refreshing the palate.

Acid also works to preserve a wine, helping it to age gracefully.

Receptors for acidity are concentrated on each side of the middle of your tongue, so that's where you should focus, especially during the attack phase of tasting.

The most prominent forms of acids found in wine grapes are malic, tartaric, and citric. The combined total of these acids are referred to as total acidity or T.A. The usual range of total acidity in dry table wines is about .50 to .90 by volume.

Malic is the most powerful of the acids; it's the one found in unripe apples, for example.

Tartaric is the most abundant of grape acids. Some winemakers will perform a function called cold stabilization to remove excess tartaric acid from white wines. The wine is put into a temperature-controlled stainless-steel tank, and the temperature is turned down to about twenty-eight degrees Fahrenheit for a period of a few days to two weeks. The tartaric acid will change from solution or liquid form to a crystal form and drop to the bottom of the tank. The reason a winemaker may prefer cold stabilization is that if a wine that has not been stabilized is kept in a cool environment over an extended period of time, some of the tartaric acid may begin to crystallize in the bottle. Some con-sumers may find this unattractive or be confused as to the wine's quality.

If you happen to encounter a wine with these "wine diamonds," as they are sometimes called, on the bottom of a bottle or even on the end of a cork, remember that they are odorless, colorless (in white wines), and tasteless, and will not harm you in any way, nor will they affect the quality of the wine.

An interesting note is that the tartaric acid that's removed from a tank of wine can be sold to spice companies who will purify it, grind it into powder, and package it as cream of tartar.

Citric acid—the one found in citrus fruits such as lemons, grapefruits, limes, and oranges—is also present in grapes.

Lactic acid does not naturally occur in wine grapes

but is created during a secondary bacterial fermentation that converts the harsh malic acid into soft lactic acid (lactic acid is the one found in milk). Besides lowering the total acidity of the wine this "malo-lactic" fermentation process also gives the wine a softer texture; it also imparts a buttery flavor and aroma.

All red wines go through malo-lactic fermentation, but only select white wines do. Sweet white wines or those with low total acidity could be ruined by malo-lactic fermentation.

TANNINS

Tannins are chemical compounds that are found in all plants. Wines receive their tannins from the skins, seeds, and stems of grapes as well as from contact with new oak barrels.

Tannins are perceived on the palate as tactile (like the dryness in the mouth experienced when drinking green tea, which is caused by tannins) and contribute to a wine's astringency, thereby affecting the wine's texture and mouth feel. Sometimes tannins may cause a wine to appear bitter (which can be a good thing) if it affects the spot on the back of the tongue where bitterness is perceived.

Tannins will also fix the color of a new wine and help it to age. They are more abundant in red wines because red wines are fermented with their skins and seeds, which release their tannins during the fermentation process.

In red wines, tannin molecules will eventually combine with color molecules and fall to the bottom

of the bottle, creating what we call sediment. Consequently, as a red wine ages, it will contain less tannin and color.

SUGAR

Without sugar there would be no wine. Yeasts eat the sugar in grape juice and convert it into alcohol and carbon dioxide (more on this on page 25).

As acid can mitigate sugar and make it taste less sweet, so sugar can take the edge off a very acidic wine.

Sugar also helps a wine age and adds to its body.

Receptors for sweetness are concentrated on the tip of the tongue. Most people will begin to perceive the sweetness of a wine when the residual sugar is between .33 and .50 percent by volume.

ALCOHOL

Alcohol is what makes a wine a wine.

The official range of alcohol content in table wines is between seven and fourteen percent, although it is not uncommon these days to encounter table wines at fifteen percent and above.

Alcohol will add size and heft to a wine as well as help it age.

Too much alcohol will make a wine appear hot or burning to the palate and the olfactory system. High concentrations of alcohol, such as in brandies or whiskies, will taste sweet.

DID YOU KNOW?

A glass of red wine contains about 150 calories.

All brandies are distilled wines, and all whiskies are distilled beers.

CHAPTER FOUR

SETTING UP A WINE TASTING

Why a wine tasting?

The obvious answer is that a wine tasting is its own excuse. It's a great way to join with friends and share in the pleasures of experiencing a common interest. In this way it's very much like a book club. And, like a book club, there are also practical advantages of participating in a group. In each instance you can learn a great deal from the insights of others, and this never changes. Experienced wine professionals appreciate the insights of other professionals, even if they disagree. So the opportunity to learn is greatly enhanced in a group tasting.

One advantage that wine professionals have over wine consumers is the opportunity to taste lots of wines in a controlled setting. The main obstacle for most consumers is sheer economics. It costs a lot of money to taste through the latest releases of Chianti Classico or classified Bordeaux, for example. But there is economic strength in numbers. If the costs are shared by several people, the opportunities to sample wines are greatly increased. You may never pay over a hundred dollars for a bottle of Opus One, for example, but if a number of people share the costs, this rare wine becomes quite affordable.

Tasting Notepads

Regional Map
Table Cards

Tasting Guide

Canvas Wine Bags

Flavor Wheels

Using Your Kit: A Basic Overview

The following is a list of items included in your kit, along with short explanations of their use. As you explore the rest of this chapter, you'll learn in greater detail how you and your guests will use these items in your tasting.

Canvas Wine Bags: Use these bags to hide the identity of the wines when you're pouring.

Flavor Wheels: Tasters may refer to these for help in describing the smells and tastes of a wine. There are six flavor wheels included in this kit.

Regional Map Table Cards: Use these maps as a visual aid when you and your guests are tasting wines from around the world. The back of the first card is a quick-reference tasting guide, which will help tasters keep track of which wine they're sampling. On it are abbreviated descriptions of each step of the tasting process, which will remind you and your guests how to get the most out of your experience with each wine.

Tasting Notepads: There are tasting notepads for both red and white wines. During the tasting, you and your guests can tear one sheet for each wine you taste from the pad and record your notes on it. You can then use the sheet for reference during your discussion.

Choosing a Theme

To take full advantage of tasting with a group, it's good to choose a theme. Themes can be quite broad, such as red wines under ten dollars, sweet wines, or favorite wines—a scenario in which the guests at a tasting are asked to bring their favorite wines.

Themes can also be very specific, such as Napa Valley cabernet franc from the 2001 vintage. If the decision is to go with a more specific theme, you may want to consider the types of tastings conducted by wine professionals. These can really be helpful in focusing your theme.

Blind Tasting

Virtually all wine tastings should be conducted blind. A blind tasting means that the identity of the wines is not revealed until after the tasting is complete. This prevents our personal preferences and prejudices from interfering with our judgment. It's considered the great equalizer in wine tasting and is the reason that bottle bags are included in this kit. (Aluminum foil can also work well as a complete bottle cover, though it doesn't hide the shape of the bottle). Even if you know which wines are in the lineup (though hopefully not the order), you'll be surprised at how tasting blind affects your impressions of a wine.

To ensure that each wine is actually tasted blind, make sure all identifying marks are obscured, especially from the top of the bottle. Often the shape of the bottle is a clue to the wine's identity, but there's not much you can do about that except to assign a designated pourer.

Vertical Tasting

A vertical tasting is one in which all the wines are from the same producer but from different vintages. The wines must be the same type, such as all cabernet sauvignon or all merlot. One advantage of a vertical tasting is that it helps you to better understand the style of a particular producer by comparing several of their wines.

Another advantage of a vertical tasting is to see how different vintages and age will affect a wine. Every harvest is different from any other, and it's very instructional to see how each vintage will leave its mark on a wine. You can also see how a producer's wines stand up to time. Some will improve over the years, while others may best be drunk within a few years of the vintage.

The difficulty of vertical tastings is the availability of the wines. Try contacting your favorite wineries to ask if they have older vintages. Your wine merchant may also be able to help track down wines for a vertical tasting. It is not essential to have each

consecutive vintage, so don't worry if there are a few holes in the vertical. It's not necessary to conduct a vertical tasting blind.

Horizontal Tasting

A horizontal tasting is one in which all the wines are from the same vintage but from different producers. The object here is to scrutinize a particular vintage and see how the weather during the growing season can affect the quality and character of a wine.

Horizontal tastings are usually reserved for exceptional vintages and include the wines from a specific wine region. Since the weather (the primary factor in determining the quality and character of a vintage) is different in every wine region, it would do little good to mix regions. It's not essential that a horizontal tasting be conducted blind, but it could make it more interesting.

Comparative Tastings

Comparative tastings are the most common and should always be conducted blind. These are tastings in which types, styles, regions, or producers are compared. For example, cabernet sauvignon from Washington could be tasted. Or Washington cabs could be tasted against California cabs. Or cabs from all over the world could be compared. The combinations are endless.

Other Theme Considerations

Although this suggestion is by no means required, it can be fun to assign one or more persons the job of researching the theme of the tasting and then sharing their findings with the group. For example, if the theme is a comparative tasting of Chianti Classico wines, someone could research such basic information as grape varieties, methods of production, and pertinent wine terms that may appear on the label (Riserva, Normale). This information can add a great deal to the understanding of the wines.

Another idea is to occasionally invite a guest speaker to your tasting. Ask the salesperson at the wine shop where you bought your wines or the sommelier at one of the better restaurants in the area. If you're lucky enough to live near a winery, perhaps the winemaker would agree to make an appearance. Often these people are flattered to be asked and even consider it good business to oblige.

Selecting and Purchasing the Wines

Now that the theme has been chosen, it's time to select the wines. The first decision to be made is how much money everyone is willing to spend. A frank discussion here is essential.

The next decision to make is the number of wines to be tasted. A manageable number is six to eight wines. Remember that the wines will be spit and not swallowed, so no one will be drinking six to eight glasses of wine. This number of selections should be sufficient to get the information you expect from the theme. Any fewer may not be enough for a true comparison, and any more could be too much for the palate to handle.

You should then decide who will purchase the wines. Most often each person or couple brings a bottle to the event, but there are other options. It may be easier for one person to gather all the wines from one wine shop. This is a good way to go if the names of the wines won't be divulged until after the tasting. This works especially well if the host chooses the theme and selects the wines. It's also a good idea if the wines are older and may contain sediment, which should not be disturbed. A bumpy ride to the tasting could have a big effect on the wine.

Serving the Wines

The Setup

Before the tasting begins, you'll want to arrange the following items from your kit on a table that is large enough for you and your guests to gather around:

• The quick-reference tasting guide

- A flavor wheel for each taster
- Tasting notepads
- The regional map table cards

You will also need to set out:

- Three wine glasses for each taster (inexpensive glass or plastic stemware is easy to find if you don't have enough wine glasses to accommodate all of the tasters)
- Pens or pencils for note-taking
- Receptacles in which tasters can spit out the wine

You may also consider setting out some food (see page 68 for suggestions on what to serve) and drinking water to cleanse the palate. Unless you're conducting a tasting that is not blind, you'll want to keep all of the wines out of sight.

The Order

The order of serving the wines is usually not an issue unless you're conducting a vertical tasting. Then the older wines should be tasted first. The reason is that older wines can be more delicate than younger wines, which can have lots of tannins and fruit. The younger wines will simply overwhelm the older ones. If both dry and sweet wines are being tasted, it's very important to taste the dry wines first, or they'll be greatly disadvantaged by the sugar in the sweet wines.

Flights

A flight is a wine term for a course of wines. A flight can be as few as one wine, or as many as ten or twelve. Wines are often broken up into flights of three wines each, making the task of tasting several wines more manageable. Your kit starts you off by providing two wine bags, making it possible for you to begin serving the wines at your tasting in flights of two wines at a time. If you'd like to include more wines in the flight, use foil or a paper bag to obscure the bottles. To serve the flight, place each wine bottle in a wine bag, and bring them out for pouring. Once everyone has had a chance to taste each of the wines in the flight and record their notes, return those wines to hiding and bring out the next flight. Generally you will not want to reveal the identity of all of the wines until the end of the tasting.

Flights can also be used if there are specific wines within a group that need to be compared with each other rather than with the rest of the wines. For example, if three red Bordeaux wines were in a tasting of cabernets from around the world, it might be more instructional to taste them together.

How Much Wine?

Each glass should contain enough wine to properly smell and taste the wine. Usually between one and two ounces is sufficient. A standard 750-milliliter bottle contains twenty-five ounces of wine, so it's conceivable that twenty or more tasters could be served from one bottle (although six to ten people is a more manageable number for most wine tastings). So, one bottle per selection is usually plenty of wine for a tasting. However, if food will be served later (it usually is), then you may want another bottle of each to drink with the food.

Temperature

Temperature is very important when tasting or enjoying wines. A wine that is too cold will be tight and closed in, and unable to release its aromas and flavors. Wine that is too warm will be too powerful and seem overly alcoholic. Often white wines are served too cold and reds too warm. Though it's difficult to assign an exact temperature for every wine (and even more difficult to attain and maintain that temperature), there are certain guidelines for serving temperatures: White wines should be refreshingly cool but not icy, which means a range of about fifty degrees Fahrenheit to fifty-five degrees Fahrenheit. Red wines also should be cool and refreshing in the mouth. There is nothing pleasurable about a tepid, "room temperature" wine. Sixty to sixty-five degrees Fahrenheit is just right for red wines. Sparkling wines, however, can be served quite cold since they are produced to be served cold. But even sparkling wines can be over-chilled. A good temperature for bubbles is about forty to forty-five degrees Fahrenheit, which is slightly warmer than your refrigerator. Ice buckets should only be used to bring a wine to temperature. They should never be used to store a wine while it's being consumed. Keep in mind that the temperature of the wine will change as it sets out, so it may need to be adjusted.

To Breathe or Not to Breathe?

That is a good question. Oxygen is the best friend and worst enemy of wine. It's what allows a wine to age and to develop complexities and nuances and

DID YOU KNOW?

Madeira wines are made by exposing them to heat for up to twenty years. Once bottled these wines will live virtually forever.

The fortified wine called sherry gets its name from the Spanish town of Jerez de la Frontera.

reach its full potential. It's also the factor that ultimately does a wine in.

While in the bottle a wine has little contact with oxygen and therefore changes slowly, but when the bottle is opened the aging process is greatly accelerated. The amount of acceleration depends on the quantity of air introduced to the wine and the character of the wine itself. When the cork is withdrawn from a bottle of wine, the amount of air that actually gets absorbed is very little since the surface area exposed to the air is only about the size of a dime. But if the wine is poured or decanted into another vessel, the wine sops up large amounts of oxygen quickly.

Any wine, red or white, that has been cooped up in a bottle for several years will definitely benefit from a breath of fresh air. It allows the wine to relax and open up. So, should the wines be opened and allowed to "breathe" before being tasted? The best approach is to open all wines just before tasting. It's very instructional to see how a wine changes and evolves as it absorbs oxygen and, consequently, how our impressions of the wine also change. Therefore, we should be prepared to alter our conclusions of a wine as the tasting progresses. Another reason not to air out a wine before tasting is that we may not know how much air each wine can absorb before it stops improving and begins to deteriorate. One wine in the lineup may be getting better while another is fading fast. This is especially true with older wines. Very old wines should be uncorked, poured, and tasted immediately. Any pleasure they may have offered can

fade within a few minutes, leaving only an acrid skeleton of the wine's former self.

Decanting

Decanting is simply pouring a wine from one vessel into another. The reasons for decanting are either to remove the wine from any sediment on the bottom of the bottle or to give the wine large amounts of air before it's served. With many exceptions most wines don't throw enough sediment to require decanting. As for aerating a wine, the most efficient method is simply to pour the wine into glasses. The wine is exposed to more air than in a decanter (especially if it's occasionally swirled), and it gives tasters the opportunity to see how the wine evolves as it absorbs the air.

So for most wine drinkers, decanting shouldn't be an issue. Besides, those things are a bear to clean.

Food?

Food can greatly affect wine, so it's important to be careful about what foods are served during a wine tasting. The safest approach is to not include food at all during the tasting, and then later enjoy the wines and food together in a more relaxed social setting. Bland crackers or breads are fine to serve for nibbling between tastes to "clear" the palate. Sometimes raw celery sticks are served to refresh the palate and clear away the accumulated tannins that can build up during red wine tastings. However, the best palate cleaner is still a nice sip of water.

Highly flavored breads or crackers should be

avoided, such as those containing caraway seeds, or spices. If cheeses are served, they should be mild with no flavorings such as smoke or hot peppers, which tend to mask wine's subtle expressions. Fruit is best not served, since it contains quite a bit of sugar, which can dramatically affect the wine.

Because the flavors, textures, and aromas of food can be distracting, it's suggested that none be served during the tasting; however, it's definitely recommend that all the wines be sampled with food once the tasting ends. After all, a wine's ultimate job is to perform well at the table. It's very instructive to see how the personalities of the wines change as they're paired with food. And also to see how the food changes as it combines with the wine.

Rating the Wines

Before you actually taste the wines, it may be a good idea to have a discussion as to how the wines will be assessed. You'll want to make sure that everyone understands the steps in the tasting process (a simplified version of which appears on the tasting guide card for easy reference) so that each taster can approach each wine in the same manner. This way, neither the wines nor any of the tasters are at a disadvantage. But there are different ways of using the information you glean from the wines.

Point Systems

Some tasting groups like to use a point system to assess each aspect of a wine. When completed this looks rather like a report card with a number grade

for each of such things as color, aroma, and flavor. The taster then adds up the grades to arrive at a total score for the wine.

In the so-called Davis scorecard, which has become an industry standard for scorecards, the total perfect score a wine can achieve is twenty. A really lousy wine would receive a grade of eight or less. Wines in a tasting can then be ranked by adding up the scores or grades given by each taster. There may quite likely be ties.

Another method is the hundred-point scale (just like the grading system used in most schools), whereby a wine is given an arbitrary overall score of, supposedly, between one and one hundred. This is the ubiquitous and controversial scoring system used by most of the national wine press. Any wine receiving a score of ninety or above is rated "outstanding" and will instantly be cleared from the shelves by eager consumers. A score of eighty-nine, however, gets little reaction from wine drinkers and is jokingly referred to by winemakers as the "nice try award." The reality of this system is that no wine ever receives a one or a twenty or even a forty-nine. So in reality, it's a fifty-point scale. A wine that receives a score of between fifty and fifty-nine is actually considered "undrinkable." A rating doesn't get much lower than that.

Ranking Wines

Some tasting groups prefer to rank the wines in order of preference to see which wine came in first. But with this and other ranking systems, there are problems, the first of which is that if you have a winner, then you must have a loser. A wine tasting should not be a competition like a horse race or a beauty contest. Instead, wines should be appreciated for their appropriateness.

There is an appropriateness about wines just as there is about food and even clothes. You may look fabulous in your custom-tailored tuxedo or a designer dress, but you would still look silly if you wore it to a picnic. It just wouldn't be appropriate. Nor would prime rib be appropriate at a movie theater, or popcorn at a state dinner. If we can look at wines this way, there is little need to have winners and losers. Rather, we would focus more on when and how we would serve a particular wine. For this reason, the tasting notepads included in this kit are arranged to prompt tasters to record their thoughts on a wine rather than rate it.

Still, if you choose to use one of the point systems mentioned above, or invent one of your own, there is plenty of space on the notepads in your kit for you and your guests to record a point score for each wine.

Discussing the Wines

Taste, Then Talk

It's best to suggest that everyone taste the wines without comment until the group is finished gathering their impressions. When everyone has had ample time to taste the wines and record their notes, the discussion can begin. You may wish to discuss each flight individually, or you may choose to wait until all the wines have been sampled and discuss all of them at once. Again, the wines are usually not unveiled until they have been fully discussed.

Everyone Speaks

A good way to begin the discussion of each wine is for one person to give their assessments of the wine, and then the next person, until everyone has had a chance to say their piece. This allows everyone an equal voice and prevents the strongest personalities from dominating the discussion.

Trust Your Palate

One of the most difficult obstacles for novice tasters is to learn to trust their own palates. This phenomenon seems to be unique to wine. If anyone was given a spoonful of sauce and asked their thoughts, there would be no shortage of opinion. It needs salt, it's too strong, it's too thick, it lacks flavor, whatever. But put a glass of wine in front of someone and ask for an opinion, and the person draws a blank even though the exercises are very similar. Perhaps it's the fear that others may disagree. But if that were a legitimate fear, there would be no wine tastings at all. In matters of taste, everyone's opinion is valid. In fact, novices can have refreshing and often more relevant impressions of a wine, because their palates are not cluttered with prejudices and biases. So go ahead and put your opinion out there and encourage your guests to do the same.

Don't Forget the Fun

When planning a wine-tasting party it's important to remember that this is foremost a social event. Second, it's an opportunity to enjoy and learn more about wines. Don't make it so complicated or serious that the event gets in the way of the fun. Sure, there has been quite a bit of information presented here, but the reason is to show the possibilities and certainly not to suggest that everything in these pages needs to be implemented to have a successful wine-tasting party. Wine tasting is like gardening in that you can put as much or as little effort into it as your time, initiative, and budget allow.

WINE SPEAK
A GLOSSARY OF COMMONLY USED TERMS

Acidity: The acid content of a wine. Acid is the nervous system of the wine and one of its most important components. It gives wine its tartness and liveliness. It also helps preserve a wine as well as mitigate the sweetness of wines with residual sugar.

Appellation: (aa-puh-LAY-shun) *(Appellation d'Origine Contrôlée)* French system of defining the place of origin of its best wines (and other agricultural products) and then controlling the standards for production as well as protecting its trademark. The U.S. version is American Viticultural Area (AVA).

Body: The weight and heft of a wine in your mouth, often determined by viscosity or thickness of a wine, which may be caused by high sugar or alcohol content.

Botrytis cinerea: (bo-TRY-tus si-NEAR-e-uh) A sometimes beneficial mold referred to as "noble rot." It attacks grape skins, causing the moisture to evaporate and the grape sugars to concentrate. It also imparts a honeyed and pleasant moldy-like smell and flavor to the wine.

Brix: Method of measuring sugar in grape juice and wine. Named for the man who developed the calibrations on the hydrometer used by American winemakers for this purpose. Degrees Brix translates exactly to percent of sugar (e.g., 20 degrees Brix = 20% sugar).

Brut: (broot) Term for driest level of sparkling wines.

Champagne Method: The original method (from the Champagne region in France) used to create sparkling wine by causing a still wine to ferment a second time in the bottle.

Clean: A fresh-smelling and -tasting wine with no off odors or flavors.

Closed: Tasting term applied to a wine that is showing little or no aromas or flavors.

Complex: Tasting term for a wine that has many layers or nuances of aromas and flavors. One measure of a good wine.

Corked: Term for foul smell and taste in a wine caused by a cork contaminated by the chemical TCA (trichloranisole). A "corked" wine may smell and taste of mold, mushrooms, wet cardboard, or a damp basement.

Crisp: Tasting term for a wine with a pleasant, refreshing amount of acidity.

Dry: A wine that has no discernable trace of sweetness.

Dumb: (See *closed.*)

Enology: (e-NAH-luh-gee) The study of wine, specifically the study of winemaking.

Estate Bottled: A wine made from grapes grown by the producer of the wine. The wine should also have been made into wine and bottled by the producer on the premises.

Fermentation: Process whereby yeasts feeding on the sugar in grape juice (*must*) secrete enzymes that create ethyl alcohol, thereby turning the liquid into wine.

Filtering: In winemaking, a method of clarifying a wine by mechanically pumping it through a filter of some sort. (Compare with *fining*.)

Fining: In winemaking, a method of clarifying a wine by adding a coagulant to the wine, which collects impurities as it settles to the bottom of the cask or tank. (Compare with *filtering*.)

Finish: The flavor a wine leaves in your mouth after it has been spit out or swallowed. It's experienced on the back of the palate.

Flabby: A derogatory term for a wine lacking sufficient acidity.

Herbaceous: (er-BAY-shus) The smell of plants, typically grass or hay, in certain wines including Sauvignon Blanc and Cabernet Sauvignon.

Hectare: (HEK-tar) The European metric equivalent of 4.5 acres.

Lees: (leez) The debris of fermentation, including dead yeasts, that collects in the tank or barrel.

Malolactic Fermentation: (mah-lo-LAK-tick) Secondary fermentation whereby bacteria convert harsh malic acid (found in green apples) into soft lactic acid (found in milk). The process softens a wine and gives it a buttery character.

Must: Term applied to the juice of crushed grapes until it has been fermented into alcohol.

Nose: The smell or aroma of a wine.

Oxidized: A wine gone bad because of too much exposure to oxygen.

Racking: Most basic way of clarifying wine after fermentation, whereby the lees are allowed to settle and the clear wine is transferred to a clean tank.

Residual Sugar: Sugar remaining in a wine after fermentation.

Sparkling Wine: Any wine with bubbles.

Still Wine: A wine that contains no bubbles.

Sur Lie: (soo-ER lee) French term ("on the lees") for aging a wine on its lees, which have the potential of imparting complexity to the aromas and flavors of a wine.

Tannin: (TAN-in) Phenolic compound found in all plants that comes to wine through grapes and new oak barrels. Affects mouth feel and texture of wine imparting a dry, chalky sensation and sometimes bitterness.

Terroir: (tehr-WAHR) French term for describing the environment in which a wine was produced and how well the wine reflects that environment.

Varietal: The character of the particular grape from which the wine was made, which shows itself in the wine's flavor or aromas. Also, the name of the predominant grape used to make the wine.

Viticulture: (vi-tuh-CUL-chur) The study and practice of growing grapes for wine.

Vitis vinifera: (vi-TEASE vi-neh-FAIR-ah) The grape species cultivated for making wine.

ABOUT THE AUTHOR

RICHARD KINSSIES has been a wine journalist since 1976 and the wine columnist for the *Seattle Post-Intelligencer* since 1982. He is a features writer for *The Wine News*, a national wine publication and the author of *Seattle Epicure,* a book on dining in Seattle.

Kinssies is an experienced wine educator. He is the director of the Seattle Wine School, which he founded in 1981, and teaches a wine curriculum for the Seattle Culinary Academy as well as a wine professional certification program for the Washington wine industry. He has also been retained by the French government to educate the wine trade on the wines of France.

Kinssies, who has been a sommelier and a wine retailer, has traveled extensively to all of the major wine regions of the world and is frequently a judge at national and international wine competitions.

PHOTO CREDITS

Date Tasted
....

Winery (name/location)
....

Special Designation (reserve, special bottling)
....

Vintage   Grape or Blend
....

Price   Color
....

Aroma
....

Taste
....

Overall Thoughts
....

WINE NOTES

WINE NOTES

Date Tasted
....

Winery (name/location)
....

Special Designation (reserve, special bottling)
....

Vintage   Grape or Blend
....

Price   Color
....

Aroma
....

Taste
....

Overall Thoughts
....

Date Tasted

....

Winery (name/location)

....

Special Designation (reserve, special bottling)

....

Vintage   Grape or Blend

....

Price   Color

....

Aroma

....

Taste

....

Overall Thoughts

....

WINE NOTES

WINE NOTES

Date Tasted
....

Winery (name/location)
....

Special Designation (reserve, special bottling)
....

Vintage .... Grape or Blend
....

Price .... Color
....

Aroma
....

Taste
....

Overall Thoughts
....

Date Tasted

....

Winery (name/location)

....

Special Designation (reserve, special bottling)

....

Vintage   Grape or Blend

....

Price   Color

....

Aroma

....

Taste

....

Overall Thoughts

....

WINE NOTES

WINE NOTES

Date Tasted
....

Winery (name/location)
....

Special Designation (reserve, special bottling)
....

Vintage .... Grape or Blend ....

Price .... Color ....

Aroma
....

Taste
....

Overall Thoughts
....

Date Tasted

....

Winery (name/location)

....

Special Designation (reserve, special bottling)

....

Vintage   Grape or Blend

....

Price   Color

....

Aroma

....

Taste

....

Overall Thoughts

....

WINE NOTES

WINE NOTES

Date Tasted

....

Winery (name/location)

....

Special Designation (reserve, special bottling)

....

Vintage   Grape or Blend

....

Price   Color

....

Aroma

....

Taste

....

Overall Thoughts

....

Date Tasted

....

Winery (name/location)

....

Special Designation (reserve, special bottling)

....

Vintage   Grape or Blend

....

Price   Color

....

Aroma

....

Taste

....

Overall Thoughts

....

WINE NOTES

WINE NOTES

Date Tasted

....

Winery (name/location)

....

Special Designation (reserve, special bottling)

....

Vintage   Grape or Blend

....

Price   Color

....

Aroma

....

Taste

....

Overall Thoughts

....

Date Tasted

....

Winery (name/location)

....

Special Designation (reserve, special bottling)

....

Vintage   Grape or Blend

....

Price   Color

....

Aroma

....

Taste

....

Overall Thoughts

....

WINE NOTES

WINE NOTES

Date Tasted
....

Winery (name/location)
....

Special Designation (reserve, special bottling)
....

Vintage   Grape or Blend
....

Price   Color
....

Aroma
....

Taste
....

Overall Thoughts
....

DATE TASTED

....

WINERY (NAME/LOCATION)

....

SPECIAL DESIGNATION (RESERVE, SPECIAL BOTTLING)

....

VINTAGE   GRAPE OR BLEND

....

PRICE   COLOR

....

AROMA

....

TASTE

....

OVERALL THOUGHTS

....

WINE NOTES

WINE NOTES

Date Tasted

....

Winery (name/location)

....

Special Designation (reserve, special bottling)

....

Vintage   Grape or Blend

....

Price   Color

....

Aroma

....

Taste

....

Overall Thoughts

....

DATE TASTED
....

WINERY (NAME/LOCATION)
....

SPECIAL DESIGNATION (RESERVE, SPECIAL BOTTLING)
....

VINTAGE   GRAPE OR BLEND
....

PRICE   COLOR
....

AROMA
....

TASTE
....

OVERALL THOUGHTS
....

WINE NOTES

WINE NOTES

Date Tasted
....

Winery (name/location)
....

Special Designation (reserve, special bottling)
....

Vintage   Grape or Blend
....

Price   Color
....

Aroma
....

Taste
....

Overall Thoughts
....